CONTENTS

FOREWORD

Exploring The Group — Opening It Up To The Global Perspective.

"When we started I thought I knew all the answers. I now realise that I wasn't necessarily asking the right questions."

Who We Are

- ★ teachers and headteachers
- ★ multicultural topic group members
- ★ staff development co-ordinators
- ★ development education workers
- ★ multicultural resources centre staff
- ★ section 11 teachers
- ★ ethnic minorities librarian

brought together by INSET co-ordinators in Kent County Council

"Development Education is not the exclusive property of any one elitist group — nor is it confined to the formal sector — it is an integral part of life."

Why We Got Together

CWDE had produced a booklet of suggestions for teachers in 1979 which has been very popular over the years. However, it was felt that, with the many new developments that have taken place in the field of education, the time had come to rewrite it. Since it was to be a handbook for teachers, who better to write it than a group of people closely involved with and experienced in classroom practice.

For some years, Kent has adopted a strong policy on multicultural education and there is a great interest in development education in the county. Contacts were made, a group of teachers in North West Kent became involved, and the project was adopted as part of their In-service programme.

£4.95

T ... OL

"Tl

...
interdependence of individuals groups and nations;

"Better Schools" 1985 para 44.

PHOTOGRAPHS

Primary Schools: The Classroom in the World

Farming: The World in the Classroom

This group was only one of the fifty curriculum task groups which meet together regularly at North West Kent Teachers' Centre, to identify needs, examine issues of common concern, plan INSET activities and engage in a wide range of group-initiated tasks.

This INSET strategy is based on the belief that teachers develop both personally and professionally when they become actively involved in their own learning. Much effort is directed into the establishment of an atmosphere of mutual support openness and encouragement in order to enable the participants to achieve their learning goals, evaluate their experiences and set new goals for the future.

Many have found that taking responsibility for their own learning and working collaboratively is more difficult than "expert-led" forms of INSET but it has helped them to develop a deeper awareness and understanding of their own learning progress which in turn has resulted in an improvement in the quality of opportunities provided for the pupils.

How We Worked

"Involvement in the group enriched my experience, initiative and approach. It has given me the strength and support to continue working for better understanding and overcoming prejudice inequality and injustice."

The original idea was for a core group to do the bulk of the writing with an outer core group to bounce ideas off and a fringe group to test and trial practical suggestions. Membership of the different groups was determined by the amount of time each individual felt they could commit to the project. This proved in the end to be a fine strategy because it did not exclude people who felt at first they had less to offer — whether of time or experience.

In fact, the core and the outer core groups merged because practically there was a need to share information and the learning process. Also, and equally important was the recognition that the group had joint ownership of the project; no one wanted to be left out. Each of us had something unique to contribute.

"Being aware of the relationships between different groups in the World is a big idea to grasp! But it starts by being aware of relationships within your own group. I learned a lot in this group. Working together we learn together."

What We Did

Initially, the group was 'obsessed' with abstract definitions of our own specific areas and with trying to establish an order of priority — multicultural education, development education, global education, environmental education — what are they? Which is most important? How do they relate?

"I never thought we'd get it together. At first we all seemed to be saying or wanting different things. I'm delighted to have been proved wrong."

It was only by working together, through the application of our diverse knowledge and skills to concrete practical classroom ideas, that we were able to establish ourselves as a bonded group: our diversity had become a strength rather than a weakness. By opening our minds to a variety of perspectives on every issue, we could see how we were each contributing to the same end: good education. Coming from a practical rather than a theoretical base, we were well motivated to write this book and to share our discoveries of methods and ideas with others, who, like us, may at times have felt ill-equipped and therefore reluctant to tackle such emotive issues.

"If this totally mixed group can work together then there is hope for the world."

A QUESTION OF IMAGES?

★ How does a child begin to learn about the world?
★ What are the strongest influences in building up a picture?
★ What distortions and confusions are created?

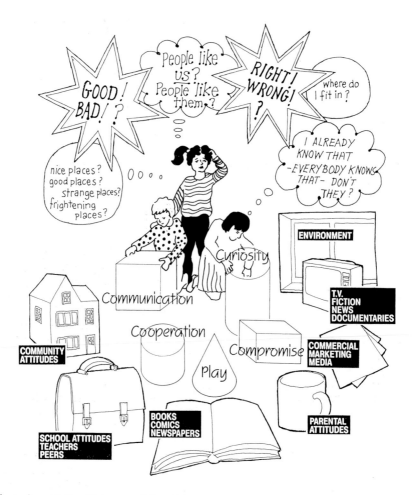

What should the Primary School be doing to equip children for life in the Changing World? The following list of aims and objectives may help you reconsider your own. They may seem rather remote and abstract, but nevertheless they should provide some signposts through the day-to-day concerns of teaching with a global perspective.

AIMS	OBJECTIVES
Knowledge *to increase children's knowledge and understanding of the world and the interdependence of its peoples.*	*for children to explore their own and other cultures and recognise diversity in society. *to find out about economic, cultural and ecological interdependence. *to understand the inequalities within and between countries and why they exist.
Skills *to stimulate enquiry and to develop an appreciation of the rapidly changing world through observation and experience.*	*to enable children to assimilate and evaluate information and attitudes from all sources. *to increase children's ability to form and communicate opinions. *to make children aware of the value of the contribution they make within their community.
Attitudes *to develop a greater awareness of the values of all people; to recognise and overcome prejudice and stereotyping; to appreciate an ability to influence the future*	*to encourage children to become more aware of their own responsibilities to one another and to the local and wider community. *to foster a greater respect for the positive aspects of their own and other cultures. *to develop empathy with and sensitivity to the experiences and rights of others, both locally and globally. *to encourage children to become aware of and to question their own attitudes.

. . . Knowledge, Skills, Attitudes.

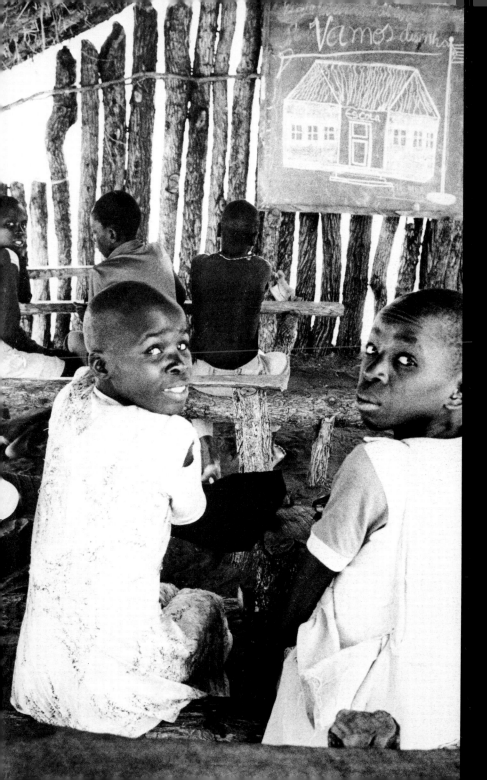

A VIEW FROM THE STAFFROOM

This short play raises some of the points made by critics of the global approach to education in the Primary classroom, and some of the responses to them. The purpose is to generate further thought and discussion by individuals and groups about the various reactions this approach generates.

Characters

Joan	— Mid 50s	Senior Teacher, Deputy Head
Tony	— Late 20s	Teaches 11 year olds
Christine	— Mid 30s	Teaches Reception
Ruth	— Early 20s	Probationer
Anila	— Early 40s	Teaches Junior

Room for development?

Scene
Primary School staffroom at lunch break. Ruth and Christine are sitting on easy chairs, chatting quietly. Tony is seated at one end of a table marking exercise books. Anila, at the other end, is reading and preparing a lesson.

JOAN	(Entering and pinning a notice to Noticeboard) Another in-service course!
TONY	(Looking up) When?
JOAN	(Peering at notice) All day Saturday on the 24th May ... that's, let me see, five weeks from this Saturday. I don't imagine **that'll** be oversubscribed.
CHRISTINE	Oh, I don't know. It depends what it's about.
JOAN	(Unpinning the notice again. Reads) 'The World in the Classroom: the Classroom in the World'. (Aside) Trendy title! (Reads) 'Teaching the Global Perspective in Primary School' ... 'Workshops on Development Issues' (Looks up) Whatever that means!!
RUTH	Ah, Development Education. We had a one-term course on that at College. I really enjoyed it. The tutor was keen and I found it exciting.
ANILA	We did very little of that sort of thing when I was at College.
TONY	Development Education? What's that?
RUTH	That's just the thing. It's not easy to define. My own view is that it's to do with looking at the way the world links together ... you know ... people, the environment, economics, trade, aid ... that sort of thing. In our College course we did a lot about developing countries and our connections with them.
TONY	(Groaning) Oh, not the Third World again!! The kids are fed up with the problems of the poor countries ... poverty, famine, war, starvation ... year after year the same old story with no improvement. Appeal after appeal ... and no amount of money seems to help. Quite frankly **they've** switched off! **I've** switched off! You just exploit the kids' sensitive feelings by making them feel guilty about the world's problems. What can **they** do? What can **anybody** do? Money in a collecting tin can't salve a guilty conscience? So why bother?

CHRISTINE	I wouldn't go as far as that. But it would seem that famine in Africa has become just another fact of life ... like the TV set in the corner. Besides, the Third World is too remote ... too far away. It's not relevant to our children.
RUTH	But it is relevant! And getting more and more important! We all live on the same planet. We trade with other countries. We depend on the developing countries for so many everyday things ... and they depend on us. Whatever affects them will sooner or later affect us ...
ANILA	... and surely it is our duty, as teachers, to help children to understand the reasons behind the situation in poorer countries. It is important that we encourage social awareness and responsibility in children.
JOAN	Well I think all these issues ... poverty, death, starvation, etc. are too sensitive to be tackled with young children. You could stir up a hornet's nest and inflame prejudice. What's more, I'm sure the whole picture in the so-called Third World is not as bad as it's painted.
CHRISTINE	That's right. You only seem to get news of disasters. Is there nothing but doom and gloom to report?
ANILA	Well, that's just it. It's the old problem of combatting stereotypes. And if teachers don't do it, I don't know who else will. It's all a question of balance. Helping children to make sense of the problems that do exist. But also to understand that there's a lot being done by the people themselves to change things.
RUTH	I also think it's important to handle sensitive issues, so that prejudices can be confronted and dealt with.
TONY	I can see that all this may be relevant in a multi-cultural school. But I don't think teachers in all white schools will think it necessary.
JOAN	Hold on Tony. I've got to disagree with you on that. Britain is a multicultural society with strong international links. Whether we like it or not, that's not going to change.

14

RUTH	Yes ... and it's important to promote tolerance and understanding between people of different cultural backgrounds. Otherwise we're storing up more problems for the future.
ANILA	Exactly! It all has to do with values and attitudes ... co-operation to bring about change ... working towards a fairer world and a more equal sharing of the world's resources. Development Education's about all of this.
JOAN	All that sounds far too political and controversial for me. I'd rather stick to the more traditional approach, concentrating on knowledge and basic skills.
TONY	I agree. This Development Education stuff seems to offer far too much opportunity for biased teaching.
ANILA	(Getting agitated) Not at all. You know as well as I do that the emphasis is on child-centred learning in Primary schools these days. This guards against indoctrination by the teacher. Children make their own evaluations. And surely basic skills, as you call them, should include the ability to assess and criticise.
RUTH	Besides, good Education is balanced learning and I believe that **Development** Education is good Education. (Thoughtful silence)
CHRISTINE	Don't you think that children of Primary age are a bit young to understand these issues? I certainly don't think that my 5 year olds could cope. It's better left to Secondary.
RUTH	(Amazed) Christine! Are you trying to tell me that young children aren't already receiving impressions of the world around them at the age of five and trying to make sense of them? They're bombarded with images ... TV, comics, etc. It doesn't take a child long to work out what's fair and what isn't.
ANILA	And that's not all. Children are so open at this age. They need information to give them a wide basis for thinking and understanding so that they can develop balanced attitudes. It has to start here in the Primary school.

CHRISTINE   I can see what you mean, but I just don't know enough about it all. I'm very unsure of how to approach it ... I don't feel confident enough about tackling it with a class.

ANILA   You're not the only one. I feel the same. But I've tried out one or two things quite successfully with my own classes. After all, good teaching is supposed to be a process of exploration for both pupil **and** teacher.

TONY   But is there any material available to help us? And are there any materials for using with the kids?

RUTH   I know of some resources, but there must be a lot more. Well there's one way to find out. I'm going to this workshop on the 24th. Anyone coming with me?

Follow-up Activities for In-Service and Pre-Service Training

1. Identify and list the criticisms of the global approach in Primary schools raised in the play.

2. Add to the list any other criticisms that come to mind.

3. Match each criticism with a justification given in the play, and answer the additional criticisms identified.

4. Discuss the effectiveness of each justification. Do they adequately answer the criticisms? Are there other, better arguements to counter the criticisms?

5. Analyse the attitudes of each of the characters at the beginning of the play to the in-service course on 'Teaching the Global Perspective in Primary School' Do these change by the end?

6. Many of the characters make statements which can form the basis for further discussion: eg.
   "The kids are fed up with the problems of the poor countries..."
   "The famine in Africa has become just another fact of life..."
   "I don't think teachers in all-white schools will think it necessary..."
   "Development Education is good education..."

A WHOLE SCHOOL POLICY TOWARDS EDUCATING FOR A CHANGING WORLD

Although many individual teachers are interested in teaching about world development in their own classrooms, how much more effective it would be if all the teachers in a school introduced this dimension into their teaching. Children from the age of five would then be exposed to a continuous thread, a spiral of reinforcement, of global ideas rather than the piecemeal approach, which allows for little continuity and often leads to confusion.

Obviously, a framework of support needs to be constructed, if the whole staff of a school is going to feel happy about teaching with the global view which is essential if we are to prepare children for life in a changing world.

The first step must be the formulation of a **Whole School Policy** towards teaching the global development perspective in the curriculum. This is the foundation on which such a framework will rest. One or two motivated staff may make the initial moves to start the process, but it is clearly important that all members of staff contribute to the discussion and share in the decision-making, so that they will have an interest in ensuring the success of the policy when it is implemented.

What follows is a description of the process which one primary school in Kent went through to formulate a Whole School Policy towards educating for a Changing World. In this case it was the headteacher who made the initial move, but clearly any member of staff can start the process:

One School's Experience

Aims and Objectives:

This school, like most, has a statement of its aims and objectives. Some time was spent examining this to identify which of the aims and objectives recognised the school's responsibility to share in the preparation of the child for life in a changing world. These were then brought to the attention of the staff, who were asked to consider whether the school as a whole, was adequately fulfilling them and, if not, how this could be achieved.

Review and Evaluation of Existing Practice:

It quickly became apparent that as a first step it was necessary to review and evaluate what was already going on in the school. This exercise gave an opportunity to identify and celebrate good practice.
The starting point was consideration of the question "What do we want to give to a child to prepare that child to become a citizen of the world?" Working in groups, so that every member of staff contributed, an agreed list of "hopes and aspirations for the child" was drawn up and arranged in order of priority. The second stage was to look at several aspects of school life in the light of the school's stated aims and objectives: classroom practice; school documents; assemblies; school rules; concerns that have engaged both children and teachers; and use of resources (time, human resources, materials). Each small group of staff took one of these aspects for consideration — the task being to identify:

(i) three examples of good practice;
(ii) three proposals for action
(iii) three areas on which the staff could work together.

By setting the statements put forward in the first exercise against the results of the second, it was possible to analyse the needs, hopes and expectations in the light of current practice.

Statement of Intent

At this stage, a brief working statement of intent was prepared. It incorporated those aims and objectives which related to the child in a changing world; described briefly current practice; and outlined the hopes and aspirations of the staff. This was helpful, since it focussed attention on what could realistically be examined, developed and put into practice within a given time scale.
Once the statement had been accepted by the staff, and in order to ensure that the staff had indeed ownership of what was being done, wide-ranging discussions took place:

— realistic targets for implementation were agreed as was a time scale.
— how responsibility was to be shared was decided upon.
— a mechanism for communication and feedback was determined and procedures for discussing problems laid down.
— workshop and other input needs were identified.
— structured agendas for meetings were settled.
— decisions were reached on how discussion documents would be initiated.

Planning

In planning the policy, the following items were included for consideration:

★ objectives — are they specific/attainable/short term?
★ research — what information is needed to proceed?
★ consensus — if what is proposed is not fully endorsed and resisted, how can this resistance be identified, and reduced or removed?
★ cost — what investment is being asked of the school by embarking on the proposed policy?
★ resources — what are the resource implications in terms of time. people (skills, knowledge, in-service) materials?
★ organisation — what expectations do the proposed course of action place on people in terms of their roles and responsibilities?

Implementation

As implementation went ahead, evaluation took place:

— is implementation working as intended?
— what lessons are to be learnt from what has happened so far?
— what criteria should be used to judge the success of the work undertaken?
— what is the next phase in the development of a whole school policy?

This, of course brought the project full circle.

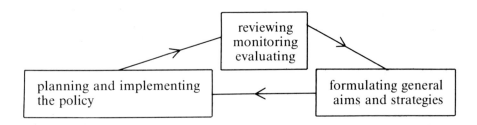

The school's policy became refined as it moved through this cycle of implementation.
The factors which in the end contributed to the successful implementation of a policy in the school towards educating for a changing world were:

★ commitment on the part of the staff.
★ a sense that the project belonged to the staff.
★ a feeling that individual contributions were valued.
★ a well informed staff.
★ adequate provision in terms of time, space and resources.
★ a raising of the status of the subject in the eyes of both the teachers and the pupils.
★ support of the Local Education Authority.
★ availability of in-service training.
★ networking between schools and other organisations.
★ informed interest shown by parents, governors and others in the project.

Results

As a result of this approach, the school reviewed its curriculum documentation. The selection of themes for projects began to reflect an increasing concern for wider issues. Attitudes in the school began to change and it became acceptable to share concerns for people in a variety of situations. A community programme developed which allowed the youngest children to show that they cared for other people. One group produced a magazine which reflected a number of points of view about a local issue. An older group followed an aid programme through its difficult path and, in an 'editorial', summarised the progress of the project and gave an opinion on its success.

A child visited Armritsar with her family and persuaded her father to come into school and share his impressions of the visit with her classmates. Another took delight in sharing her family's loyalty to the memory of Gandhi. This led her class into a consideration of the events surrounding India's struggle for independence and into an attempt to understand the viewpoints that emerged at that time.

The project theme 'Holy Places' was chosen to give the children the opportunity to meet people of different faiths and to find out something of the significance of the faith to the believer. In each of the holy places visited, worshippers spent time with the children explaining why particular aspects of the place of worship were important to them.

Some children made a video film in an attempt to explain the reasons for famine. Through the making of the film, their understanding grew. When they shared the film with others, they demonstrated an empathy with those who were suffering and when their efforts were applauded, they replied that they didn't want praise, only understanding for those who suffered.

Conclusion

Throughout, the stress was on the value of the contribution of each individual on the staff and on the fact that the ownership of the outcomes rested with the whole staff. This approach did work and whether you are an individual or a group of concerned individuals, you can take heart from the fact that well laid plans did succeed.

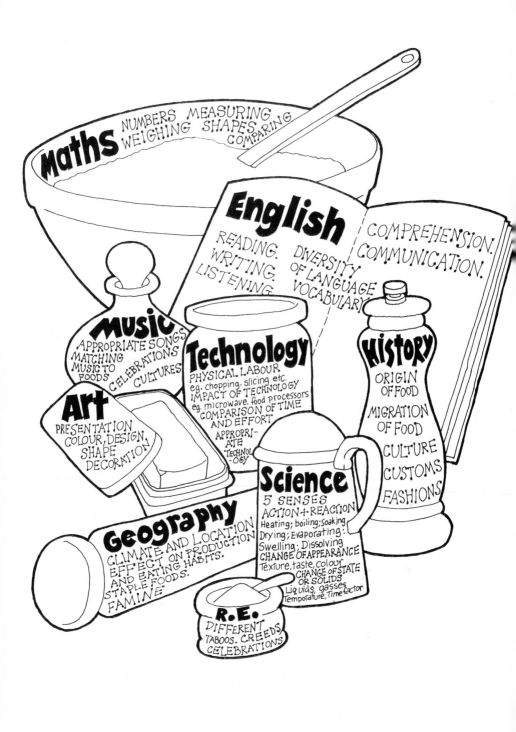

THE WORLD AND THE CORE CURRICULUM

The National Curriculum

In the Primary School the national curriculum will include, in addition to Religious Education, nine foundation subjects of which the first three are to be **core** subjects:

English	Technology	Art
Mathematics	History	Music
Science	Geography	Physical Education

"The main aim is a national curriculum that is a framework not a straitjacket . . . it will be for schools to decide how the curriculum is to be organised and taught . . . They will choose whether or not to use subject headings for their timetables; they might prefer to use a thematic or modular approach where they believe it to be appropriate" DES 1988

Most primary school teachers balance the topic approach, which crosses the curriculum, with work which focusses on specific subject areas. Often the boundaries between these approaches overlap leading to integration. The global dimension is not a separate entity; it permeates the whole curriculum. We discuss later, how a topic can be opened up to explore this dimension. Here, our concern is to show how a subject orientated curriculum can be broadened out and linked with the wider world. Subjects can cover aspects of topic work relevant to themselves. For example, a whole maths lesson could be built around one aspect of a topic on food, where fruit and vegetables are arranged in sets. (p59) 'A Recipe for Real Understanding' on p76 shows how a recipe can form the basis for exploring global links in each of the foundation subjects. It might not be immediately obvious to choose a recipe as the basis for a History lesson, but a closer look will reveal that a recipe can provide a medium to explore several themes: e.g. original food sources; how these have changed and why; cultures, customs and fashions in food through the ages.

The following table lists some of the activities suggested in the lesson plans on Food, (part IV) and how these are relevant specifically to the core curriculum.

Curriculum Area	Activities	Skills	Global Links
MATHEMATICS	Sorting food: fresh/processed; thick/thin skins; colour; size; shape. Graphs: likes/dislikes Distributions: where different foods come from.	Gathering; Sorting; Recording Interpreting	Adaptation to conditions and needs. Countries of origin.
	Sharing: dividing food among class. Comparisons: heavy/light; large/small.	Division Weighing Measuring	Worldwide distribution of food. Fairness. Interdependence.
	Party Planning: shopping; preparing; cooking.	Estimating Money Weight Capacity	Sources of food Harvesting Festivals Shopping and cooking in other countries.
	Clearing up: water quantities involved; left-overs; time taken.	Capacity Checking estimates Time	Waste Pollution
LANGUAGE	Accounts: preparing for celebration/festival, and the part food plays.	Imaginative Writing	Empathy with other cultures
	Discovering local sayings dialects and	Vocabulary	Regional variations of

SCIENCE		
variations in meanings in connection with food.	Speech	language in small areas.
Poems, stories and rhymes about food locally involving multicultural and language aspects.	Literature	Links to other countries and origins.
Growing food: from seed to crop.	Observation Testing: grow similar seeds in various conditions.	Conditions necessary for crop growth. Why crops fail in some areas.
Preservation/deterioration: subjecting food to various conditions.	Testing Observation	Variety of means of preserving and storing food.
Materials: shape/materials of cutlery, utensils, crockery, etc.	Testing for thermos properties; durability; shape.	Varying needs/availability.
Senses: presentation; effect of appearance, smell, texture on our taste. Colour/aroma tests.	Awareness of co-ordination of senses	Likes/Dislikes National/International Dishes/Flavourings.

WHAT DO WE MEAN BY . . .

Content, Process, Concepts, Knowledge, Attitudes, Skills, Evaluation?

These words crop up again and again in books on Education so it is important, for the purpose of this book, that we define them. It is too easy to assume we understand them, but jargon often takes over and creates, at worst an exclusive rather intimidating aura, and at best a fuzzy way of thinking, based on the assumption that we all share a similar understanding!

CONTENT	— The Subject/Topic/Theme.
a) TOPIC	— The specific subject to be explored, e.g. Food.
b) THEME	— The thread running through a topic, or linking Topics together.
PROCESS	— The activity or method used to explore the Content.
CONCEPTS	— The formation of an idea, an understanding.
KNOWLEDGE	— That which is learned, whether factual, conceptual or skill based.
ATTITUDES	— The way we view something, often reflected in our behaviour.
SKILLS	— Specific abilities, (physical and intellectual), acquired through learning and developed by practice.
EVALUATION	— A means of assessing the development or attainment of content, process, concepts, knowledge, attitudes and skills.

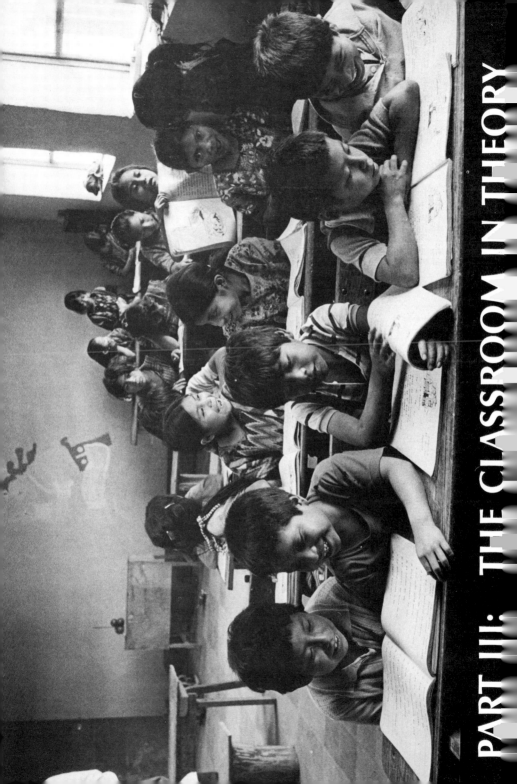

PART III: THE CLASSROOM IN THEORY

CHOOSING YOUR TOPIC ...

Although it would seem ideal if topics arose directly from children's interests, in reality the classroom teacher has to make the final decision in order to achieve a balance and meet the demands of the education system. But the children's interests should remain a major consideration since without their curiosity and co-operation, topic work becomes dull and routine.

The diagram illustrates some of the topics that can be explored, with reference to the child's own immediate experiences. For example, the topic of Shelter on a global scale can be related to the child's own home and neighbourhood, even play, experiences and linked to those concepts appropriate to the age group.

Using APPENDIX 1, a Topics and Concepts "ready reckoner" can be constructed. By superimposing the three independently moving circles (experiences/topics/concepts) it is possible to line up and identify those themes to be explored:

For example:

ME → MY HOME → SHELTER → SIMILARITIES/DIFFERENCES.

CONCEPTS IN TOPIC \

Matching Content with Process

Why should topics be organised around concepts? In ⌐   ⌐ this question, let us consider what a concept is. A concept i   abstract or general idea. Concepts serve as tools, or symbols, by which we can share meanings. When we are very young, words such as 'co-operation' are incomprehensible to us. As we grow older we begin to understand that this 'label' stands for a whole system of meaning that we can all recognise.

Concept based education could be described as a journey. If you imagine the vehicle to be the content, the road as the process then the traffic signs and our developing attitudes and responses to them become the concepts.

If the vehicle is not appropriate we will have a bumpy and uncomfortable trip, it is also unlikely that we will arrive safely at our destination. So we have to match the vehicle to the relevant transport system. You cannot drive an express train along the M1! It is also essential to recognise and respond to the signs along the way. Observing the 'Highway Code', is crucial if the journey is to be a safe and enjoyable experience.

Looking at the list of concepts (page 32) we might well ask, 'How can we teach such abstract ideas to the very young?' Young children cannot conceptualise abstract ideas. Of course we cannot 'teach' a concept, but we can structure an activity so that various chosen concepts will be experienced along the way. Five- to six-year olds need very concrete information with which to work. They need to be able to relate to that information and explore it from the security of their own experience.

There are a number of concepts that can be used as foundations for topic work in primary school. Similarities and differences, social change, co-operation, conflict, fairness, interdependence are all appropriate. In the years before children start school, they will already have had a wide variety of experiences. When children enter school, teachers should help them make sense of their personal experiences. This can be done by organising topics around chosen concepts and approaching them in an open-ended way. For example, a teacher can build into a topic the concept of Co-operation by choosing a process in which the children work in groups, helping each other, working together, exchanging and exploring ideas. If the concept is Fairness then the process should have advantages and disadvantages built into it so that the children experience 'fairness' at first hand. They can then explore their feelings of anger, envy, guilt etc. in the security of a game or class-lesson. They can also look for realistic solutions to these issues without feeling threatened or overwhelmed by the size of the problem.

At this stage of early learning the process is as important as the content because the concepts are only apparent through the process; they are inextricably linked. We would not expose a learner driver to the hazards of the fast lane until they were totally secure on familiar, safe and well sign-posted roads.

What we are doing is suggesting basic ground rules, a 'Highway Code', which by constant application to games, activities and classroom practice, will become second nature. If we concentrate on fostering such concepts as Co-operation, Fairness, etc. we will be giving our pupils those skills and tools that will help them throughout life to make total use of shared resources, resolve conflicts, and form decisions based on discussion, tolerance and consensus.

Children forget facts from one lesson to the next, but the building up of concepts, skills and attitudes based on experiences, images and impressions becomes an indelible part of the thought process.

As we know children often learn by osmosis. They are capable of absorbing and exploring what we, as adults, would see as very complex issues. Yet such issues are not the exclusive property of 'grown-ups'. The difference is that we theorise about them — children live them. Once children have learnt to assert themselves, to recognise that they each have something unique to contribute towards the whole, they can then progress with confidence, to look beyond themselves to the wider world. They will have acquired those skills and attitudes which are necessary for them to later address complex, global issues in the secure knowledge that they can play a useful, active role as members of an interdependent, changing world.

They will have passed their 'driving test' and be ready to explore exciting, new roads, with confidence.

AGE	CONCEPT	
5-7 YEARS	CO-OPERATION	FAIRNESS: COMMUNICATION: SIMILARITIES & DIFFERENCES:
7-9 YEARS	INTERDEPENDENCE	UNEQUAL DISTRIBUTION: CAUSES & CONSEQUENCES:
9-11 YEARS	VALUES AND BELIEFS	CONFLICT: SOCIAL CHANGE:

The grid shows a list of key concepts appropriate to a child's understanding at a given age. No matter which concept is being focussed on many others will inevitably crop up — for example, we cannot fully explore 'Co-operation' without experiencing some areas of Conflict, Communication, Fairness, or even Social Change. It is tempting to get side-tracked, but unless we bring the focus firmly back to the key-concept it could lead to confusion.

At a later stage of development children can tackle those more sophisticated concepts such as Social Change, Values and Beliefs, etc. head-on and will be bringing with them an understanding of Co-operation, Fairness, Causes and Consequences, etc. as useful tools. In this way each concept will be experienced at all levels but only focussed on when they are appropriate to the child's degree of understanding.

A SIMPLE SPIRAL APPROACH

"We begin with the hypothesis that any subject can be taught effectively in some intellectually honest form to any child at any stage of development. It is a bold hypothesis and an essential one in thinking about the nature of a curriculum. No evidence exists to contradict it; considerable evidence is being amassed that supports it."

J. S. Bruner.

The learning skills of a child grow and develop throughout their schooling and continue to develop throughout life, so it is important that the knowledge, skills, attitudes and concepts the child develops are positive, free from prejudice and relevant to the inter-dependent world society in which we live.

These skills and concepts are constantly changing. So the approach to learning must be flexible whilst remaining appropriate to the child's ability at any given stage of development.

By adopting a simple spiral approach we are planning a system of reinforcement, whether of knowledge, skills, attitudes or concepts, which builds and grows around the child, and therefore, no theme or concept will ever be exhausted.

The topic might not be exhausted but . . .

These ideas are not necessarily new, but they are now more possible to implement with the move towards an integrated team approach to staff development being adopted by many primary schools.

The teacher works as an enabler; encouraging curiosity, teaching those skills and providing access to such knowledge, as is necessary to satisfy that curiosity. At the same time the teacher will be learning to adjust to the needs of the children.

Constant evaluation is essential. Without this it is impossible for the teacher to identify those areas which require reinforcing — when to proceed up the spiral, and when to recap, stand still, or even re-work an aspect of the theme. Ideally the spiral will be widening from the base as the child's knowledge and understanding increases. It may even be necessary to go back down the stairs. It is also important to have some feed back from the children as to their understanding of the concepts being explored. By adopting this two-way evaluation process we can realise the child's full potential and achieve our learning goals.

OPENING A TOPIC TO THE GLOBAL PERSPECTIVE

So, if we choose 'shelter' as our topic, it is not by looking at how other people build their homes that we introduce a global perspective it is with the recognition of shelter as a basic human need. When we move out to look at how different people make shelter we balance the similarities of needs with the differences. If there are inequalities in the provision of shelter we need to develop an awareness of why such inequalities occur. Taking this approach, all topics have a global relevence running through them. The global perspective is not something tacked on to the end of a project, nor is it a mystical, distant goal. It is simply a way of seeing the world as 'One World'. We live in one world and unless we view it as a whole we are omitting an essential part of the equation. By dividing and isolating a 'First World' from a 'Third World' we loose the bonds and connections which exist in world relationships and will not be viewing the world as interdependent, a place where every activity is inter-related.

We do not have to look hard to find the global perspective, it is everywhere. It is not 'geography', it is about those links which exist between human beings living on this small planet. It is about developing concepts and attitudes which foster an awareness of inter-dependence; that people depend on each other for the satisfaction of their mutual needs. We are not saying that every topic should cover the whole world but that there will be, within each topic, some aspects which mirror the wider world.

These aspects can be developed in many ways. The concepts we are concentrating on include similarities and differences, co-operation, fairness, interdependence and conflict solving, all of which are universal, and can be fostered in activities which are not obviously global. But they do lay the foundations for a deeper perception when the theme is widened out to bring in experiences which focus on other parts of the world.

We have to start with the experiences of the child. These experiences are universal (see diagram Choosing a Topic), and can be transferred later on to a direct global aspect. The concept of people being different yet similar at the same time is one that can be fostered within the classroom itself.

But, children soon become aware of the wider world via television. The fact of differences is clear enough but, how do we develop sympathetic attitudes? Do we despise the poverty that exists in the world? How do we answer the questions about why there are inequalities and differences? We cannot know everything about the world, nor cover every culture and every country. But we can study how people behave in various circumstances and why things happen. What we are trying to achieve is an understanding of a situation and to avoid an attitude of condescension and superiority.

Often problems do not have simple answers but this need not prevent us from exploring some of these issues with our pupils. An important aspect of the 'Global Perspective' is to develop an awareness that there are different points of view and that there is not always a final answer.

'Knowing by Doing'

Many simulation exercises have been devised to facilitate this exploration process. Through simple role-play games pupils experience what happens when they become farmers or traders; when they start to buy and sell or feed themselves and their families. Concepts can be explored by the simple re-organising of classroom work. Collaborative methods of work; sharing, discussing, experimenting all build up an awareness which is global in its implications. Simulation games take this one step further, by easing the children, through their imagination, out of their normal environment. Activities which have an unequal distribution of resources and encourage children to make decisions and choices, resolve conflicts and reach consensus, help them to understand some of the ways that people relate to each other in the world at large.

These activities do not need to be 'foreign' in order to be 'global'. An awareness of local issues can be helpful in giving young children some experience of decision making, with an understanding of the implications those decisions may hold for themselves and others. A simulation exercise about a local road scheme can be transfered, later in their spiral progress, to an airport development project in West Africa. It is the process, the dealing with a situation or problem, which is important.

Active learning — 'knowing by doing' — is a device which allows children to reflect on their intentions, their activities and the resulting outcomes. The children are becoming aware of open-ended, inquiry based issues and learning to view themselves and others from a different perspective — not by leaping into the unknown, but by a logical process of simple comparison.

PLANNING A TOPIC: FOUR MODEL QUESTIONS

Having chosen your topic, brainstorming is a good way to clarify ideas and bring out new aspects which might otherwise be overlooked. Brainstorming can be done by yourself or with the children. Write down everything, sensible or not, that could be explored in the topic then gather ideas into groups — headings usually suggest themselves, and a web is soon produced.

There may not be time to explore every possible avenue, but select a range of themes that gives a balanced view of the topic. Ways should be found to introduce and expand the global perspectives which already exist in every topic, linking them to the child's immediate environment. Global issues cannot be taught in isolation. This 'one world' approach is essentially good teaching practice. It should be natural to the teacher to discuss the global aspects of all classroom work being undertaken by the children of all age ranges every day.

In testing the above criteria for preparing the classroom activities on Food, the writers, as a group, followed the brainstorming procedure to its conclusion.
What emerged were four core questions (refined from an original six) which when answered covered the whole topic area.

1. **What is it?**   **(definition)**
2. **Where does it come from?**   **(origin)**
3. **Why do we need it?**   **(need)**
4. **What do we do with it?**   **(use)**

Taking it further, it was realised that these questions formed a model, which applied as much to other topics as it did to Food.

Storage:
Long Term: Preservation — freeze; can; dry; salted; process.
Limited Term: Stocks of — cattle; sheep; chickens; fish.
Short Term: Fresh — cool store.

Preparation:
Cooking: gender roles; recipes; restaurants.
Convenience Foods: fads; waste; packaging; preservatives.
Celebrations: taboos; religious observances; ritual; sacrament.
Methods: frying; boiling; open fires; roasting; microwave; knives and forks; chopsticks.

Use:
Social: family meals; school dinners.
Celebrations: parties; weddings; funerals; religious occasions;
Cultural: cultural diversity; availability; climate; similarities.

Quest

FC

Brains

WHA

Sensation:
taste; smell; touc

Type:
fish; meat; egg
pulses; cereals; swee

Nourishment:
vitamins; protein

Energy:

Sacrament:

EED IT?

mine; disease.

alth food; sugars;
ditives; allergies.

eparation.

rvation: malnutrition.

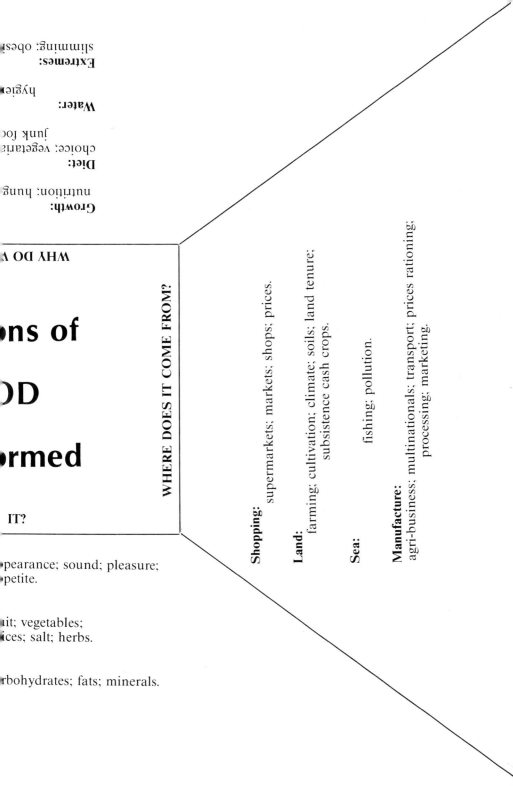

Extremes: slimming; obes[e]

Water: hygie[ne]

Diet: choice; vegetari[an]; junk foo[d]

Growth: nutrition; hung[er]

WHY DO [Y]

ns of

OD

rmed

IT?

pearance; sound; pleasure;
petite.

it; vegetables;
ces; salt; herbs.

rbohydrates; fats; minerals.

WHERE DOES IT COME FROM?

Shopping: supermarkets; markets; shops; prices.

Land: farming; cultivation; climate; soils; land tenure; subsistence cash crops.

Sea: fishing; pollution.

Manufacture: agri-business; multinationals; transport; prices rationing; processing; marketing.

EVALUATION

The purpose of evaluation is to gauge the appropriateness and effectiveness of a course of learning.

Here we are concerned mainly with the evaluation of learning episodes which take place in the classroom. This starts with the setting of aims and objectives which become the yardstick against which progress should be measured.

If classroom aims and objectives are set out with the broad aims and objectives of this book (p9), clearly in mind, then the evaluation of each learning episode, project or activity, will allow an overall assessment to be made in the long-term.

(Practical illustrations of evaluation are contained in the chapter on Classroom Activities. Part IV.)

Classroom Evaluation

The questions listed below could be used as a guide to monitor the effectiveness of a project, class activity, etc. They can be used as planning aids or as a means of evaluating the **CONTENT** and **PROCESS** for both the teacher and the pupil.

Before: What do I/we want the outcome to be?
What do I/we need to know?
How can I/we go about this?
What resources do I/we need?

During: Are the children actively involved, interested?
Does the process match and compliment the content?

After: If I/we did this activity again, what would I/we do differently/the same.

Outcome

Evaluation of knowledge/skills, through testing, multiple choice, problem solving, etc., is well chronicled elsewhere. **Our** objectives are organised around key concepts which concentrate on attitude and behaviour. Evaluation of these needs to be approached in a more open-ended way. Observation, experience and 'gut feelings' are the main tools for the evaluation of attitudinal changes and the developing conceptual awareness of our pupils. There are guidelines and techniques which are helpful in this context:

For example:

		Evaluation Techniques
CO-OPERATION	— working collaboratively	observation
INTERDEPENDENCE	— sharing, fairness, co-operation	observation/diary role-play
CONFLICT	— ability to recognise and deal with conflict	problem solving outcome
VALUES & BELIEFS	— empathy, self esteem tolerence	(process & end product of group task)

Before and after techniques are helpful in this context:

True/False Quiz
Brainstorming
Selecting appropriate adjectives
Word association
Mental Maps
Explaining/Reporting to someone else
'Something new that I have learned is . . .'
'What I can do now is . . .'

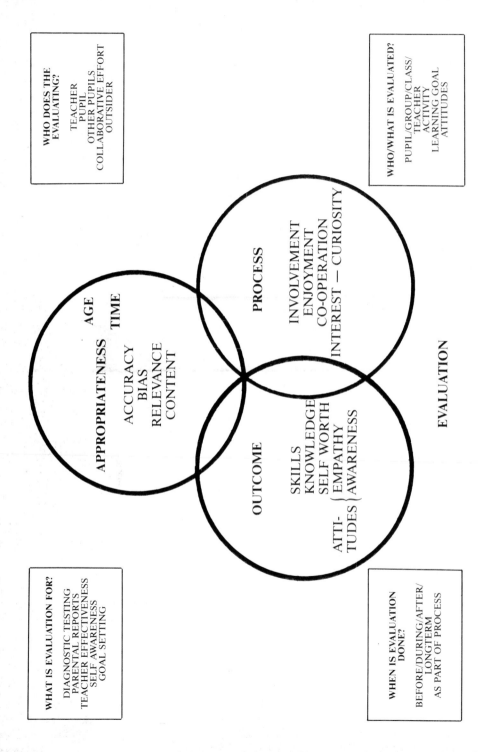

WHO DOES THE EVALUATING?

TEACHER
PUPIL
OTHER PUPILS
COLLABORATIVE EFFORT
OUTSIDER

WHO/WHAT IS EVALUATED?

PUPIL/GROUP/CLASS/
TEACHER
ACTIVITY
LEARNING GOAL
ATTITUDES

PROCESS

INVOLVEMENT
ENJOYMENT
CO-OPERATION
INTEREST — CURIOSITY

AGE
TIME

APPROPRIATENESS

ACCURACY
BIAS
RELEVANCE
CONTENT

OUTCOME

SKILLS
KNOWLEDGE
SELF WORTH
ATTI- { EMPATHY
TUDES { AWARENESS

EVALUATION

WHAT IS EVALUATION FOR?

DIAGNOSTIC TESTING
PARENTAL REPORTS
TEACHER EFFECTIVENESS
SELF AWARENESS
GOAL SETTING

WHEN IS EVALUATION DONE?

BEFORE/DURING/AFTER/
LONGTERM
AS PART OF PROCESS

44

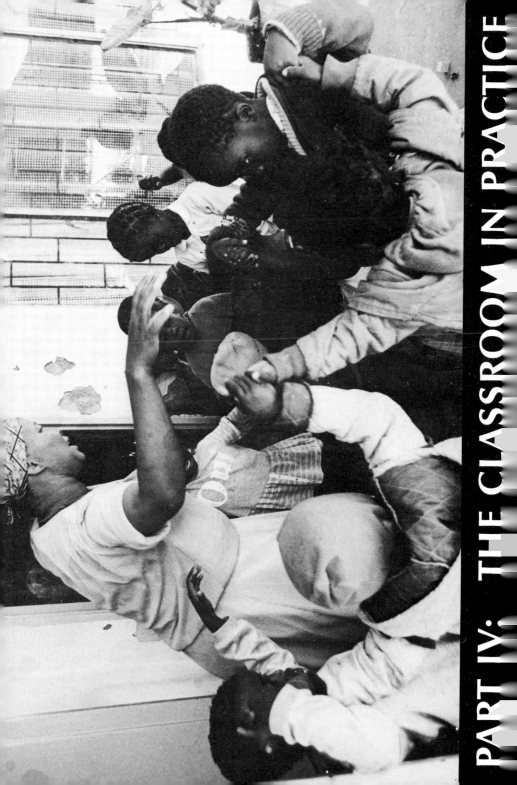

Theory is fine — but how would all this translate into practice? That was the real test.

We set ourselves the task of preparing a topic for classroom application. We felt that the thought process we had followed would apply to any topic but chose the topic of FOOD as it is possibly the most commonly worked topic in Primary schools. It was also a relatively 'safe' choice, bearing in mind that we would be trialling sometimes out of context, and with little say in follow-up work plus the fact that we did not want to leave areas of conflict or confusion for the resident teacher to have to mop up.

We were always conscious of the fact that we were not planning a complete topic. Time and circumstances would not allow for this. But we wanted to know if we really had understood the concept of opening out a topic — not just "tacking a bit about the third world on the end!"

Determined to practice what we were preaching we divided into small working groups. Each took a different age group to focus on. (5-7's, 7-9's, 9-11's)

At various stages we reported back and reviewed our work. We trialled the work in schools, on ourselves and with other teachers. The end result is three thematic approaches to the topic of food. These plans are not definitive nor are they without room for improvement, but they do work. We would expect you as teachers to adapt them to suit your class. Only you can know what your pupils are capable of — but please never underestimate them.

CONTENTS

THEME PLAN: 5-7 years
Fruit and Vegetables

Aims and Objectives

To encourage children to work in a co-operative way, by using group activities, sharing skills, helping each other, respecting each others opinions, communicating these and reaching consensus.

CONCEPTS	CONTENT/ KNOWLEDGE	SKILLS AND ABILITIES	ATTITUDES	PROCESS
STAGE 1 CO-OPERATION Communication Fairness Similarities and Differences	Variety/types of fruit and vegetables Colour awareness Numbers Senses	Sorting Collaborating Counting Imagination Decision making	Sharing Empathy Consideration Self esteem Group esteem Awareness of others	Coloured dots game Vegetable role play
STAGE 2 SIMILARITIES AND DIFFERENCES Co-operation Fairness Communication	Types of Ingredients Numbers Weights and Measures Colour Shape	Decision making Collaborating Measuring Counting Sharing skills Following instructions	Sharing Helping others Creative awareness Fairplay	Following a recipe
STAGE 3 CO-OPERATION Similarities and differences Communication Interdependence	Language Numbers Money	Decision making Negotiation Communication Collaboration Costing Reaching consensus	Giving Pride/self esteem Group esteem Group identity Awareness of others Tolerence	Planning a party
Introduction of Values and Beliefs (To be developed later)				

The Colour Game: A Simple Role Play

Method
1. Place a small coloured dot on the forehead of each child, (it is essential that they do not know which colour they are given). The class must then sort itself into colour groups (6x5). They may not talk during this game so that in order to find their own group they will have to start by helping others. This is a useful method of pre-selecting groups whilst giving the children ownership of their groups and, therefore, a sense of belonging. Try to mix abilities, gender and personalities — a little gentle social engineering!

2. Place a selection of fruit and vegetables on display e.g. Apple, Banana, Tomato, Potato etc.

3. Each group must decide collaboratively which food matches the colour of their group, i.e. Red group — Tomato. This can lead to lively discussion — if not conflict!

4. When they have all selected their food ask them to examine it and try to identify with it. i.e. are we hard, soft, heavy, light, fat, thin etc.

5. Get them to write or plan a short story to explain their life story as the particular fruit or vetegable, to the rest of the class. (By using role-play in this basic form the children are encouraged to be less self-conscious and will often express quite personal feelings which may otherwise remain hidden.)

Points to Consider

Where did they come from?
Tree, bush, ground, etc.
Who grew/picked them?
Have they changed shape
and colour as they grew?
Where could the rest of the
class find them? Shops,
garden, etc.
Have they travelled far?
Do they like hot or cold
weather?
Do they need peeling,
chopping, cooking?
Do they taste nice? etc.

Ask the Class

Ask the rest of the class to
comment or add any
information they feel has
been missed out.
At this point the theme
could be explored in many
ways. One food could be
chosen by vote (which is
most popular, useful, etc.)
and some research into
origins, etc. could be done:
e.g. Potato — History —
variety of use
Banana — Journey from
grower to fruit bowl.

*We chose to take the concept of Co-operation further by asking the
groups to mix and form a 'meal'. (Remember the concept is as
important as the topic at this age.)*

Numbers Game

1. Ask the class (still in role) to mix themselves up by running around
(always allowing for space!)

2. Call out a number and ask them to form, as quickly as possible, a
group of that number. Repeat this several times ending with the number
6.

3. Each member of the new group should have some knowledge of what
they represent. Ask them to plan a dish, or meal, (soup, pudding, etc.)
just by using the members of their group.

4. Get them to share their meal plan with the rest of the class:

Points to consider:

Was any food missed out?

If so why?

Which was the most popular, easiest etc.?

Do they need other ingredients from other groups?

5. Working in pairs, ask them to plan a dish or meal using every member of the class.

6. Ask them to describe their new form:

Questions to Ask:

Have they been changed, cooked, mashed, peeled, etc.?

How many colours are there?

Have they changed colour by mixing together?

Do they taste better when mixed together?

How many countries have they come from?

At this stage they may want to actually prepare the 'meal' — or illustrate it with a collage.

Following A Recipe

> *The next logical step seemed to be to follow an actual recipe. The recipe we chose was for Barfi — an Indian sweet — It seemed a natural choice, not because of the obvious global dimension it would introduce, but because one of our group is Asian. It is also an easy recipe which involves no cooking and shows very clearly the concept of similarities and differences by taking every day ingredients and turning them into something unfamiliar to most of us: the similarities between cultures often being greater than the differences.*
>
> *The process we used concentrated on the need for Co-operation, but this time we introduced the concepts of Similarities and Differences, and Fairness. This process could be used for any activity which has an end product.*

1. **Grouping:** Divide the class into working groups. This could be done by using a game or by letting the children chose their own groups, (a way of evaluating how much they had learned from the previous session.)

2. **Utensils and Ingredients:** Try unevenly distributing or including inappropriate items and excluding an essential one so that the children have to negotiate, discuss and eventually co-operate, in order for them all to complete the recipe. With a little imagination this normally mundane task can become an intrinsic part of the lesson.

3. **Following the Recipe:** Once they all have the correct utensils and ingredients they can work within their groups. Get them to identify their various skills and find the best way of working for the benefit of the group.

4. **Clearing up:** This is as important as No. 3, and once again should be a co-operative effort. Watch how the labour is distributed — Gender can become a big issue here. Has there been any wastage? You may want to do some follow-up work on pollution.

5. **Distributing the Sweets:** Who do they want to eat the food — The Head Teacher, families, friends, themselves? Why? Could they use it to help others — as a means of fund-raising or as community service by taking it to an Old Peoples' Home in the community etc.? Are they willing to pool their results? All suggestions should be justified and the final decision arrived at through negotiation and discussion.

(The actual recipe for Barfi can be found on p77)

Planning A Party

The children may then want to follow up their work by planning a party. This would fit well with the concept of Co-operation. You may find it coincides with a specific celebration (Christmas, Diwali, Chinese New Year) which would provide the opportunities for language development and contact between pupils and adults (helpers) of different ethnic origins and for the informal development of understanding of aspects of different cultures. (Fitting well with the concept of similarities and differences whilst introducing the concept of values and beliefs.)

1. Divide the class into groups with different tasks assigned to them. Each group would report back at intervals and the rest of the class would provide feed-back and raise issues.
(Alternatively the class could approach the project collectively.)

2. Research of the likes and dislikes of the children for whom the party is to be given and plan the menu.

3. Invitations designed and written (possibly bilingual) and numbers to be catered for decided.

4. Shopping for food etc. Group estimates amount of food required and buys it.

5. Group plans activities for party — music/decoration/dancing/games — appropriate for the occasion.
Class discuss reasons for choice.

6. Class prepares food with advice and help from adults when needed. Class discussion on utensils and methods used.

7. Class discussion on presentation — to match culture and traditions.

Evaluation of Concepts

Points to observe:

How well did they work in groups?

Did they form new groups easily?

Did this skill improve over the course of work?

Did they help other groups or compete?

Were new friendships formed?

Did the class structure alter in any way? (Very long term evaluation)

All these points and many more should be discussed with the class. If they have found it difficult to co-operate explore why — can they see ways of improving co-operation?

The class may like to devise their own question-sheet and conduct an 'in-house' survey.

NOTES:

THEME PLAN: 7-9 years
Fruit and Vegetables

Aims and Objectives

To understand the rich variety of foods
available to us.
To experience the inequalities which
exist in the production of food for
survival and health.
To foster an understanding of the efforts
of others to produce much of our food.

CONCEPTS	CONTENT & KNOWLEDGE	SKILLS/ABILITIES	ATTITUDES	PROCESS
CAUSES & CONSEQUENCES	Types & varieties of fruit & veg according to taste/colour texture/size etc.	Collaboration	Sharing (ideas, tools, skills)	Sorting
Fairness		Reaching consensus		Modelling; Drawing; Painting; Writing
Co-operation	Conditions/ requirements for growing etc. eg. soil; climate	Decision making	Empathy	
Similarities/ Differences		Experimenting	Curiosity	True/false quiz
Interdependence		Manual skills	Respect for others	Planning/devising growing conditions
	Use of tools appropriate technology	Selection & Classification	Tolerance	Practical experiment of growing food
		Observation	Open-mindedness	
	Need for food — survival/health	Planning		Map work
	Climatic variations & effects on food production	Recording		Recognising/ Monitoring/ Recording/ causes & consequences
		Evaluating		Evaluating results

What are Fruit and Vegetables?

1. Brainstorm 'Fruit and Vegetables'. Working with the whole class just list all their different ideas as quickly as possible. (Set a time limit, 2 or 5 minutes, and be sure to write down everything, without comment or censorship, on a large sheet of paper as this will be referred to later.) This is a good way to focus their minds and stimulate thought. Study the brainstorm and have a brief discussion as to how one might group the items that are listed.

2. Divide the class into small groups (6 x 5) and ask them to sort a basket/box of fruit and vegetables into sets.

> * How many different sets can they find?
> (Colour/size/shape/texture/taste/from home or
> abroad/hot or cold climate etc.)

3. Get each group to choose one set and sort their food accordingly.

4. Each group should then present their selection to the class explaining their method of work.

5. Allow for discussion about each selection and compare and contrast them.

6. The various sets can then be recorded by drawing/painting/modelling/ writing etc.

STAGE 2

Where do Fruit and Vegetables come from?

1. Compile a simple True or false chart for the class, working in pairs, to complete.

	True	False
All food is grown		
Not all plants need water		
All Plants like bright sunlight		
We only eat food grown here		
All plants produce seeds		
All farmers use tractors		

They must agree each point with their partner before they fill in their form. This creates lively discussion and feeds their curiosity to find out the right answers. (It is not a test!)

2. Having compared their quiz sheets with the rest of the class try to reach class agreement on the answers.

3. Based on the result of the quiz they should be able to identify certain criteria for growing food. Once these have been discussed and explored can each group then devise various conditions, some good some bad, in which to grow some food.

Points to Consider:

At this stage the teacher will have to guide them so that the experiment is controlled and covers the main points that you want them to explore.

eg. ★ outside: full sun/shade/very damp/very dry
   ★ inside: in a cupboard/over heat/on windowsill/in a draught
   ★ Different soils: fine/clay/stoney
   ★ Access to water: regular watering/inconsistent watering/
      drought/flood
   ★ Access to fertilisers: none/too much/regular amounts

Try to mix the conditions so that some groups have an obvious advantage/disadvantage or so that labour is not necessarily rewarded. eg. Plot 'A' might be on a windowsill, in full sunlight, with poor soil and no access to fertilisers or water. It is best to choose a crop that has a short growing season, such as radishes or mustard and cress. If the school has access to a garden plot, an outdoor crop could be grown as well. This has the added advantage of involving real weeding and digging and the fact that the growing conditions are often beyond our control, with regard to the weather, could prove an important learning point.

4. Draw lots as to which 'plot' each group gets.

Questions to Ask:

How well do they think they will do?

Do they each have the same chance?

Will some have to work harder than others — if so why?

Will hard work guarantee a good crop?

Can they think of any countries where food is grown in similar difficult conditions?

All these points and many more should be discussed and recorded before and during the growing period. There will be plenty of time during the growing period to explore different methods and conditions of farming around the world, eg. three out of four of the world's farmers are women; the need for appropriate technology; soil erosion; land distribution. Use the photos in this section of the book to explore some of these issues.

Points to discuss after the harvest:

★ Who got the best/poorest harvest?

★ Can they identify and understand why?

★ How do the results compare with their predictions?

★ Did the best harvest go to the hardest workers?

★ How do they feel about the results, are they fair?

★ If they were growing food to live on what would the consequences be?

★ Can they find any ways of solving the problems they may have identified?

★ Is this what happens in the world at large?

Who Grows the Food?

1. Return to the original brainstorm. How many of the listed items come from overseas? Locate the places on a world map.

2. Do any of them come from countries where we know some people are very poor? Does poverty make it more difficult to grow food? (cost of fertilisers, irrigation, land etc.)

3. Select one product to focus on.

Questions to Ask:

★ How far has it travelled?

★ What sort of climate was it grown in?

★ Could anyone live on this one product?

★ Would that be boring/healthy?

★ Who grew it?

★ What do they eat and where does their food come from?

---

4. Can any of the solutions discussed in stage 2 be applied here?

Evaluation of Concepts

Some evaluation is already built into this course of work

Keep diaries, individually or in groups or as a class. (Keeping all three could lead to interesting aspects of bias and vested interest through comparison.)

Match the pupils predictions to results

How well did they work together?

Did the groups help each other or compete?

Was there sympathy with groups whose harvest failed?

Was there resentment towards privileged groups?

Did they pool the harvests and share them?

Take a straw poll — was it fair?

Do the 'successful' feel this as strongly as the 'unsuccessful'?

Can they re-organise the system to be fairer?

NOTES:

THEME PLAN: 9-11 years
Lifestyles and Food

Aims and Objectives

To develop an awareness of the shared nature of humanity: To study similarities and differences in society and to foster respect and tolerence towards the values and beliefs of others. By working collaboratively, to explore lifestyles within the class, community and the wider world, with particular regard to food. To recognise individuality within groups and avoid stereotyping by so doing.

CONCEPTS	KNOWLEDGE & CONTENT	SKILLS/ABILITY	ATTITUDES	PROCESS
VALUES & BELIEFS	Food types Food values	Collaborative working	Co-operation	Brainstorming
INTER-DEPENDENCE	Processing	Sorting Selecting Comparing Cutting Pasting	Tolerance	Discussion Categorising
Similarities/Differences	Costs		Empathy	Extending group work on collage
Choice	Social structure	Decision making	Consideration	Community survey
Social change Co-operation	Social needs	Problem solving	Self-esteem Group esteem	Analysis of findings
	Sampling	Reporting back	Respect for different cultures/social groups/age etc.	Looking towards a Global Community
	Comparative study of another culture/lifestyle	Expressing opinions	Politeness and consideration	
		Recognising similarities/differences		
		Analysis		
		Interviewing		
		Communicating Monitoring Prioritising		
		Making fact/value judgements		

STAGE 1

Lifestyles — Variety and Choice

1. Brainstorm foods eaten by the class at their last main meal. (Keep this information as it will be referred to again later.)

2. Discussion on similarities and differences; choice and variety; likes and dislikes, etc.

3. Working in small groups or pairs (so that each child is more likely to contribute) ask them to choose a category and classify the food identified in the brainstorm, e.g. Food Types (cereals, fruits etc.) Food Values (proteins, vitamins etc.) Country of Origin (Home, abroad, specific countries.) Cost (cheap/expensive); Fresh or Processed etc. How many other foods can they add to their chosen category?

4. Get each group to design a collage depicting the widest possible range of foodstuffs within their category. (Using cut-outs, photos, drawings, food labels etc.)
Ask them to choose a title for their collage, and to agree it with their partner/group.
e.g. If they were studying processed food they might call their collage 'The manufacture of food', or 'It's in the Bag!'.

5. Ask each group to elect a reporter who will explain their work to the rest of the class. Allow time for questions and discussions involving the whole class.
This would be a good point to look further into the effect of food processing on cost/taste/value/environment etc.

6. Each group or pair should join with another group and find a link between their work, e.g. favourite food + food values. Fresh food + processed food. Processed food + cost etc.
By combining the two collages can they create a new title? e.g. 'Just eating what you like isn't enough!', 'The changing world of food' or 'The real cost of the package'.

7. Display all the combined collages together. Can they find one common link: identify an overall picture? e.g. they may feel there is a link between fresh food, healthy eating and good value for money. Or they may decide that processing food makes it look good but cost more.

8. Can they agree a title/caption for the combined work? e.g. 'Fresh food keeps you healthy, wealthy and wise.'

This would be a good point to look further into the effect of food processing on cost/taste/value/environment etc.

Questions to Ask:

Does the collage tell the whole story suggested by the title?

If not can they identify what is missing?

How should they fill these gaps?

9. Return to the original brainstorm and compare it with the final collage. Could they tell the same story using just the original selection?

Points to Discuss:

What are the similarities/differences between the two?

Was it a more interesting picture now?

What various stages of work had been involved?

How many times did they combine their work?

Did this improve it or not?

Could they have achieved such a complete picture working alone?

In pairs? in Groups?

Would looking beyond the classroom enrich the picture in any way?

All of these points will serve as useful methods of evaluation, not only of their understanding of the process but also of their attitudes towards group work.

STAGE 2

Community Research

1. General discussion to explore the concept of 'a community'.

Points to Consider:

Family structure: Old; Young; Babies; Income variations; Housing variations; Institutions; Disabilities; Different cultures; likes and dislikes; wants and needs etc.

2. Having defined 'community', ask the pupils, working in pairs, to select one sample group to focus on (eg. the elderly), and to compile a questionnaire with very clearly defined and specifically identified aims. e.g. is it difficult for the elderly to shop in our community? They should then conduct a series of interviews (focussing on food) within the classroom/school/community.

Points to Consider:

★ Favourite food; willingness to try 'new food'; variations in common foodstuff such as bread; where do they shop; religious taboos/customs/festivals; diets of conscience (vegetarian, vegan); diets of health (low cholesterol, diabetic) restrictions of economy, effects of advertising etc.

★ Remember questions which start with WHO, WHY, WHAT, WHERE, WHEN, will discourage 'yes' and 'no' answers!

★ How should they conduct the interviews? Politeness, empathy, and patience are important.

★ Should they use tape-recorders, cameras etc?

3. Still in pairs, write up and analyse the findings of the survey and report back to the rest of the class.

4. Whole class discussion on the overall picture.

Points to Consider:

★ Can they identify areas of need within the community?

★ Can they prioritise their findings?

★ Are they surprised at the findings?

Possible follow up work:

Using their understanding of the community and its needs, can they design an 'Ideal Store' to cater for as many of those needs as possible? (paying particular attention to the top priority identified earlier).

Could they extend the survey of lifestyles by looking beyond their community to the wider world?

STAGE 3

The Global Community

1. Write down an over-simplified statement for the children to discuss, e.g. Everyone in India eats rice.
(If you choose a cultural group that is represented in your class be sure to avoid any children feeling they have been singled out or 'picked on').

2. Working in small groups ask the following questions:

Questions to Ask:

★ Does anyone have first hand information?

★ Were any Indian people sampled in their survey?

★ What did the survey show about their eating habits?

★ Was there a wide variety of eating habits within the community?

★ Did this get broader as they looked further afield?

★ Is it likely to get broader or narrower as they look further still?

★ How would they feel if the statement said: 'All the British eat Fish & Chips'?

★ How would they feel if this was said by someone from India?

★ Do they think the statement is accurate or not and can they justify their opinion?

We now want to build on the understanding of variety within any given social group and extend this view to dispel any stereotyping of cultural groups within our own country or in countries other than our own.

3. Can the class think of ways of gathering information about food that is eaten in India?

These are just some ideas, but it is important that the children always refer back to the research work they did in their own community. Choice and variety is closely linked to economic factors.
Once the children have identified these links for themselves it would be an ideal chance to explore the links of poverty and malnutrition.

Evaluation of Concepts

Points to Observe:

How well did they collaborate?

Pupils could keep diaries of progress.

Where do they see themselves in the community?

Does the end product show concern for the needs of the community?

Is their understanding of different cultures presented sympathetically?

Has this understanding grown?

Pupil written reports on insights into community — have they been surprised? shocked? pleased? disappointed by any of their findings?

Can they see ways to improve/change/develop the situation?

NOTES:

ACTIVITY PLAN: 5-7 years
'A Recipe for Real Understanding'

Aims and Objectives:

To introduce the concept of
SIMILARITIES AND DIFFERENCES, and
reinforce concepts of co-operation,
fairness and communication.
To understand and follow a recipe.
To foster awareness of variety; equal
values within varieties; and the
enrichment of life by variety.

Curriculum:
In this instance the activity was used as a special half-day session
with a class of 6 year olds. It could be used as an integrated part of
the term's topic work (p53) or many recipes can be used as the
basis for any of the nine foundation curriculum subjects (p22)
with the possible exception of P.E.!

This recipe has been used many times with children aged 5-7 years. It is ideal for this age group as it requires no cooking or use of sharp knives. It does, however, involve lots of decorating and presentation. It may have an unfortunately high sugar content but then many developing countries have inherited a dependence on sugar as their major source of foreign exchange. Don't forget to include the added ingredients as described on p53, as these are essential to make it a Recipe for Real Understanding! These sweets could be used to celebrate Baisakhi, Diwali, Easter or Harvest.

Ingredients:
(enough for 2½lbs of barfi)

400 grms	condensed milk
500 grms	desiccated coconut
500 gms	icing sugar (sieved)
50 grms	nuts — cashews, almonds, and pistachio
10 grms	green cardamoms ground — (optional)
100 grms	diamond cut jelly sweets
1 pkt	hundreds and thousands
	food colouring — green, red, yellow
	icing sugar for rolling out
	moulds of different shapes — squares, circles etc.

Utensils:
Rolling pin, knife (not for cutting), bowls, scales, can opener, spoons.

Method:
1. Weigh and measure the ingredients.

2. Mix the milk, coconut and chosen colouring together.

3. Add the ground cardamon at this stage if desired — let the children decide — cardamons have a very strong flavour.

4. Leave to stand and harden.

5. Roll out on a board dusted with icing sugar, cut into shapes.

6. Decorate with the remaining ingredients according to choice.

(Barfi tastes like coconut-ice. By substituting 500 grms of full cream powder milk for the coconut you will get Peras, also from the sub-continent of India. Peras tastes like Milky Way.)

By following the sort of procedure explained on p53, the actual production of the sweets was a relatively minor part of the mornings work. Most of the time was spent in decision making, and negotiation — what colours should they use, what shapes, how should they be decorated? How should the labour be divided? etc. — questions which required a great deal of negotiating by the children before they could reach total agreement.

Points to Discuss:

The last part of the morning was spent discussing:

★ Which shapes were best?

★ Did the different colours alter the taste?

★ Did the shape and colour matter?

★ How should they share them?

★ Should they mix them up?

All these questions and many more form a firm foundation for important complex issues that the children will have to face later in life. Many may be facing them already, and need an opportunity to ask questions, to voice and challenge opinions, and to recognise and counter prejudice, within the relative security and disguise of a class activity.

Evaluation:

The children wrote and/or illustrated their individual accounts of the session.

1. The whole class at work.

2. Their group at work.

3. Themselves at work.

ACTIVITY PLAN: 7-9 years
Going Bananas

Aims and Objectives

To introduce concepts of interdependence, similarities and differences, justice in trade etc.

To foster NOW empathy, appreciation, fairness in everyday relationships and LATER attitudes of fairness dealing in international/cross cultural contacts.

To involve all children of a multi-cultural class in activities relevant to them at present via a familiar food stuff and to arouse interest/sympathy in rest of school plus parents etc. at the Assembly.

Curriculum

Language: Oral and Written/Research: at home and school, use of books and pictures and parental input (especially Jamaican, East African Asian children).

Maths: Drama: PE: Music: RE: Multi-cultural/World Studies.

This session was planned and used over a three week period in the mid-summer term, (near Christian Aid Week but it would be suitable for One World Week; Harvest or West Indian Festival Time), culminating in a school assembly presentation. It could be expanded/included for longer projects and adapted for other products.

What we did

* We called the end product 'GOING BANANAS'. Each child wrote an invitation to parents to attend, at the outset before any other action. The name caught their attention and led to a spontaneous Brainstorming session from which we listed: jokes, jingles, poems, a game, names of pop-groups etc. and a few facts/opinions about the actual fruits.

* All the children made larger-than-life cut-outs of bananas and discussed them as *food* preferences etc.

* We looked at illustrations, including slides (taken by a member of staff) of banana plants. We explored the variety of shape, colour, size and ways of consuming them in several places of origin.

* "Journey of the Banana" a sketch/playlet was cast and read aloud several times in class (with explanations). Obviously care was taken to avoid stereotyping when casting. This could be taped or performed live. The activity led on to finding out more about the West Indies, especially Jamaican, background. The parents of a Jamaican girl were very helpful in supplying data but they disliked the statistics on poverty of rural peasant farmers, which really brought home the fact that we were talking about real people in real situations, with real feelings.

Going Bananas Assembly

- Most of the class were seated facing the rest of the school and parents; holding cut-out bananas.

- A group playing shakers and tambourines accompanied a small group dressed in yellow jump-suits, who entered singing 'Banana Pyjamas', and doing acrobatics etc. Pairs of children told quick fire "jokes".

- A Banana Board Game (provided by a child) was demonstrated by four children.

- A volunteer quartet recited "Bananas and Cream", (provided by a child). One child ended the introductory session by asking "What about Real Bananas?"

- Question and answer dialogues were read aloud giving some basic facts about production, sale etc.

- A Jamaican girl read her own account of West Indian life based on parents' recall.

- The class performed a play using real bananas and eating them at appropriate points, and using large poster-type props showing the % of price that goes to the various contributors in the chain from planter to consumer.

- This was rounded off with a thought provoking passage, spoken by a child, on where our food comes from; people who produce it; fairness in trade etc. (Applicable to other commodities.)

- The Hymn Kumbyaya was sung by all and the children led a thanksgiving for food with prayers — selected by the children — from a book of prayers from around the world all composed by under twelves. The assembly ended with a final rendering of the Caribbean Lord's Prayer, with percussion.

Evaluation — by observation as teachers.

Continuously throughout preparation, *active participation* of all children, oral and practical. Noted confidence and pride of ethnic minority pupils who could contribute from experience or talent in class as well as the public event.

Fun/enjoyment evident in participants (2nd year juniors) and 'audience' — across age (1st-4th year + adults), ability, social and ethnic ranges.

Empathy — informal conversations of children in the class at break, lunchtime and groupwork.

Older children's *reactions*, reported by colleagues, that the point was taken about inequalities in international trade, living standards etc.

Resources

Teacher:
   World Studies 8-13 Handbook P. 56-61.
   OXFAM publications on West Indies.
   Personal slides from East Africa.

Children:
   School reference library.
   Own books.
   Banana game(s) etc. from out of school activities, Brownies, T.V.

Supplementary:
   Assemblies for Development CWDE.
   Banana Split — Christian Aid Video.
   Banana Commodity Sheet CWDE.
   Whose Gold? — Latin America Bureau (for secondary but contains useful information and can be adapted in part).
   Geest — information packs for children.

ACTIVITY PLAN: 8-11 years
Putting Food on the Map

Aims and Objectives:

To introduce the concepts INTERDEPENDENCE, co-operation and fairness.

To show the Global distribution of food, in relation to population and land mass. To explore the food we eat and think about the countries that contribute to our daily diet.

Curriculum

Geography: spatial awareness, global awareness, map-work.

Maths: proportional distribution; division; comparisons.

Humanities: sharing; group participation; group awareness.

Art: drawing; design.

You will need:

a) A large simplified Peters projection map with the North South divide shown clearly. (Christian Aid do one — we made our own floor map 6' x 4').

b) A different coloured template for each of the 8 major world regions.

c) A coloured card for each child. This card will also show their food allocation (see map and chart, appendix II).

  N. America (2)(2,5); Europe (4)(2,3,3,4); USSR (1)(3); Japan/Oceania (1)(3); Latin America (3)(1,2,4); Africa (4)(0,1,2,3); Asia (8)(1,1,1,2,2,2,2,3); China (7)(2,2,2,2,2,2,2)

d) 68 Dolly mixtures or sultanas.

e) 30 satsumas/easy to peel oranges (children can provide these).

f) 30 sheets of paper, just large enough to wrap an orange.

g) 30 felt pens.

h) A globe.

This activity day was planned for the top class of a typical, small rural Kent School. Out of a total of 100 all white pupils, 10 are travellers, a minority group who are often singled out through prejudice and fear. It was a pleasure to work in this school where the children had a sense of their own worth, and a shared appreciation of the contribution each made to the school. Being a small school, the top class ranged from 8 to 11 years (30 children).

The day was divided into two sessions. In the morning session we 'explored' the world and in the afternoon we found that world in a super market bag. It was a very full day and although it worked well as a 'one off' activity it would also form an ideal starting point as it opens up so many avenues for the children to explore. Each session could be used on their own but they complemented each other very well indeed.

Mapping it Out

1   Each child wrote or drew a picture on their sheet of paper. We then tried to wrap the oranges without destroying the image on the paper.

2   Next they drew on the oranges and a great deal of speculation took place as to what would happen to the picture when the peel was removed and put together on a flat surface. The oranges were peeled and the peel re-assembled. The children worked in small groups and discussed their findings among themselves.

(This is a lovely experiment for 5-6 year olds whose conceptions are so different. Beyond this point the exercise is too abstract for them.)

3   We then gathered round the large map. Our map just showed an outline of land mass, with the equator, tropics and North/South divide.

This group chose to call it Richer World/ Poorer World. A group of much older children were asked to rename the North/ South divide and after heated debate decided on the 'Majority/Minority' not only putting the South first but giving the North the negative image for a refreshing change. *

* At a workshop run by the Education Officer for Intermediate Technology.

Points to Discuss:

What shape is the world?

What is the difference between the flat map and the globe?

Which was land and which was sea?

What did the lines represent?

Are they all geographic lines like the equator?

If they are man-made can they and do they move?

What does 'First World' and 'Third World' mean?

Is it a good description?

How many worlds do we live in?

Could they think of a better description?

4   We then spent some time looking at ourselves.

(It is essential that the children realise the differences among their own micro-world before they can begin to understand the macro-world.)

Points to Discuss:

Do we all have the same amount of money?

What about pocket money? Paper-round earnings?

Are there some people in this country who are rich?

Are some people in this country poor?

Do we live in the Richer World or the Poorer World?

Is everyone in the Rich World rich?

Is everyone in the Poor World poor?

5   Each of the coloured templates was then held up in turn and identified. This class were very good at geography and recognised most of the regions, but this could be played as a guessing game, a sort of jigsaw, with clues.

6   As each region was identified it was placed on the map.

Ask the Class:

How much land was above the line: in the Richer World?

How much was in the Poorer World?

Which is larger?

How many of them had travell;ed to another region or country?

What was it like?

Is there a middle to the map? To the world?

(Remember the oranges. One girl said if she lived in Japan she would want to be in the middle of the map and was delighted to hear that Japanese maps do in fact show this! This is a good time to compare the flat map with the globe. Follow up work could include tracing and overlaying different map projections.)

7   The next stage was to look at relative sizes of the regions. (This is why it is important to use a Peters Projection. Although it elongates the continents, their size in relation to each other is much more accurate than on the Mercator projection.)

8   The children then placed 'Europe' and later just the UK (which came adrift on our template) on to Africa to see how many times it would fit. This led to a great deal of practical maths — and a wide variety of answers.

9   Having put the land onto the World we then looked at population distribution.

Ask the Class:

How many people are in the world?

5½ billion. Can they imagine that number of people?

Is it easier to visualise 30 people?

If our class was the whole world where would most of us live?

Did most people live in the Richer World or the Poorer World?

Which region did they think was most densely peopled?

10   Each child took a colour card. By sorting themselves into colour groups they could see which region they belonged to and find the answers for themselves.

It is important to stress that there is not just 1 person living in the whole of the USSR, and that Japan and Oceania are together to avoid having to chop someone up into smaller pieces! Each child, in fact represents approximately 180M people, so they have really to use their imaginations!

11   We then 'fed' the World, using the dolly mixtures. Each child was given the number of sweets indicated on their card. (These figures are based on the Food and Agricultural Organisation's statistics relating to grain production.)

Points to discuss:

If everyone needs 2 units of food how much do we need?

If we have 68 units of food (sweets) have we got enough?

What happens if you don't eat enough?

What happens if you eat too much?

Did we have enough food (sweets) to go round?

How fair is it?

What could they do about it?

The children were very quick to recognise a system that has enough to go round but fails to meet everyone's needs is unfair. They were not, however, so quick to share! They could also see that even within one region the distribution was uneven, or that not everyone in the Richer World had plenty nor were all the Poorer World hungry or starving. They failed to feed the class.

Points to discuss:

Why did some of the class end up 'hungry?'

How big is the classroom/the world?

If we failed to feed ourselves is it surprising many people in the world are very hungry?

The World in a Supermarket Bag

An important part of the picture was missing. We wanted to find out where the food came from in the first place. We grew it? Did it move around the world? Did those who grew it get to eat it?

To begin to answer these questions we played 'The World in a Super-Market Bag' (published by OXFAM).

This required a bit of earlier preparation but was well worth it.

1   The class was divided into groups of 5. (We mixed ages, genders, skills and abilities.) And each group received a bag of 6 items. eg. Rice from Surinam, Butter fron New Zealand, Onions from Chile, Bananas from the Windward Islands. They unpacked their bags, identified the contents, noting the price and the country of origin.

2   Each child drew a picture of their product, located it on a large wall map, and linked their drawing to the location by string.

They were also asked to consider if a product seems expensive or not and any reasons they can think of for such variations.

Once the map was completed we could see just how much of the food was produced in the Poorer World, and it was a wonderful display to use as a focal point for a whole school assembly.

The activity is very easy to follow, the instructions are clear, and the children obviously enjoyed it, while discovering a great deal about food production and distribution.

Although we packed this into one very busy, enjoyable day it might have been wiser to spread it out over a longer period for the sake of the facilitators!

By use of a simulation exercise such as this the children were actually feeling unfairness; guilt; the need to share; selfishness; interdependence; even complacency. They could see there were no simple answers, vested interest played a large part in the problem.

All of this led to a lively discussion mirroring the world situation with alarming accuracy. eg. "I'll give my extra sweets to my dog!" or "I'm not sharing with her, I only want to share with my friend!" or, "I don't like Dolly Mixtures!" (The difference between choice and survival.) There was plenty to talk about as suddenly the World really had become the classroom, and the classroom the World.

Resources:

The World in a Super Market Bag — OXFAM
Peters Projection Map — Christian Aid
Which Projection — Action Aid
North South leaflet — CWDE
Disasters pack — OXFAM

Evaluation

The children completed an evaluation sheet from the pack 'Disasters in the Classroom'. OXFAM.

Preparation and presentation to the school in an assembly.

The sessions obviously formed a framework of understanding which they constantly referred to in later learning episodes.

COMPUTER BASED ACTIVITY PLAN: 8-13 years
What Do We Eat? A Topic-based Computer Program

Aims and Objectives

To study similarities and differences by comparing diets at home and abroad. To use the information stored in the computer database. To select relevant information, understand, analyse and communicate specific chosen aspects of that information.

What Do We Eat?
A Topic-based Computer Program*

The computer has a unique potential for storing, organising and providing large amounts of useful information as and when required. It is a very valuable teaching aid.

This program fits into a classroom project on the topic of Food. It provides easily manipulated information on analysing what we eat and comparing our food with that eaten in other countries.

> *"I used the program with a group of children and indeed based a substantial unit of work around it. These were 10-12 year olds in a Middle School."*

Before any mention is made of the computer element, preparatory work in class includes: map work, and a general discussion on foods (raw, cooked, fast or convenience, packaged) and their ingredients.

The class first uses a worksheet which lists nineteen countries representative of developed and developing countries. By going through the countries with the class, using atlases and a large wallchart (preferably the Peters' Projection), the children have the opportunity to identify the country which interests them. They might have come from that country, have heard about it on television, have read about it, or have a relative there. Each child then chooses a country from the list and using an atlas finds out the region of the world the country is in, its capital city and the names of three neighbouring countries.

> *"Worksheet 1 in context was a useful lead in, providing a focus before using the program."*

A second worksheet contains instruction on how to keep a Food Diary — a record of food eaten in a twenty-four hour period. Classroom discussion on the labelling of packaged foods, the ingredients of common foods and a general awareness of food names and types helps the pupils to break down their food intake into a form required by the program.

With the information contained on their completed worksheets, the class is now ready to use the computer — to check out their geographical information, to compare their diet with that of their chosen country, and to find out about some foods unfamiliar to them.

"When the group of children had used the program and come away with a lot of information comparing their diets with a wide range of other countries, the hard part was coming to grips with this information and representing it in some meaningful ways. The question of whether the differences in what had been eaten that day across the class were significant when compared across the countries studied, occupied a lot of discussion. Each pupil produced a coloured grid of their study country indicating which foods were eaten more than (red), about the same as (green) and less than (blue) in this country. We then pinned them up on the wall in groups according to countries. When we stood back and half closed our eyes some overall trends became apparent. Things like more cereals and less meat and fats being consumed in a lot of countries only then made themselves obvious.

I believe that this is a constructive use of the micro computer — you don't have to waste time gathering data but can apply your mind to its implications."

Flowchart

From "What Do We Eat?" Booklet

What Do We Eat? was developed and published by the CWDE Computer Project.

Some Helpful Resources on Food

For Class Use:

We Are What We Eat!	UNICEF*
The World in a Supermarket Bag	OXFAM*
World Feast Game	Christian Aid*
Potato Profile	OXFAM*
Land is Life	SCIAF*
The Roots of Hunger	SCIAF*
World Food Day: Photo Pack	CWDE*
Slide Set: Nigeria: Food and Nutrition	CWDE*
Slide Set: Grounds for Hope	Traidcraft*
Banana Split	Christian Aid
Slide Set: A School Garden	OXFAM
Slide Set: Harvest from the Sea	OXFAM
Slide Set: Rice Production in Kampuchea	OXFAM
Roots and Shoots	OXFAM
Sowing and Harvesting**	OXFAM
Banana Photo Pack**	OXFAM

For Reference

Food and Nutrition	UNICEF*
Recipes from around the World	OXFAM*
Population and Food	Ed. Arnold*
Commodity Sheets:	
Tea, Rice, Maize, Sugar, Coffee, Wheat, Bananas	CWDE*
Teaching Development Issues: Food	Manchester DEP*
Just Food	CAFOD*
Food for Life	Macmillan*
Why? We ask why they are Hungry	Christian Aid*
Food Matters	Birmingham DEC*
Whose Paradise? Tea and the Plantation Tamils of Sri Lanka	MRG*
Breaking the Famine Cycle	Christian Aid*
Food: Resource Guide for Project Work in Primary and Middle Schools	OXFAM
Nutrition Guidelines	ILEA
Food as a Resource for Learning in the Primary School	ILEA

* These materials are available from CWDE.
** New publications for 1989.

Choosing Resources

There is a wide variety of resource material available to the teacher for use in topic work with a global perspective in the primary school. This includes: teachers' handbooks; pupils' books, audio-visual material (video, tape/slide, slide sets); photopacks; activity packs; posters/wallcharts; games and simulations; and computer software and of course people. Some of these materials aim to give ideas to primary teachers and some can be used directly with pupils in the primary classroom. A lot of other material is very relevant and can be adapted by the teacher for use with younger children. Many of the visual materials — photo and activity packs — and some of the games, lend themselves to such adaptation.

The use of computers is becoming an increasingly important feature of classroom practice in Primary schools. Some software programs for use in topic work already exist (p93) and others are being developed. These programs, like many other classroom resources, are designed for use as an integral part of curriculum activities.

Classroom Resources

When choosing a topic, it is always advisable first to check out available materials and to look at them. It is clearly important that teachers should know the material their children are going to use. This can be very time-consuming but is desirable since the images children can get from the resources they use in the classroom may be very misleading — stereotyped, inaccurate, condescending or deterministic. In addition it is important to know the range of material that exists since this will determine how the topic can be developed. The greater the variety of resources available, the greater are the possibilities. Many of the organisations whose addresses are listed later produce catalogues of educational materials for sale.

Apart from the school or local library and the teachers' centre, materials can often be borrowed from the multicultural resources centre, local development education centre and the aid agencies. Many librarians will co-operate in making up a Project Loans Resource Box of classroom materials which can be borrowed for a whole term.

What To Look For

In many cases the resources available from school and teachers' centre libraries will have been scrutinised to ensure that they conform to language policy standards laid down by local Education Authorities. Such policies aim among other things to select materials which reflect an understanding of the multicultural society. However, these materials and certainly materials from other sources, should be looked at to assess whether they are appropriate to the aims and objectives set out at the beginning of this book.

The following questions may serve as a 'checklist' for some of the criteria which should be considered when choosing suitable materials:

Are Stereotyped Images Presented?

Materials should give a sensitive, sympathetic portrayal of people with an emphasis on the fact that they are **real** people from a **real** place with feelings and interests. Care should be taken that the 'sample' picture built up of different groups does not lead to the assumption that all people in the group are the same. The 'travelogue' approach and caricatures of ethnic minorities should be avoided.

How Are Cultures Portrayed?

Characters from non-European cultures should not continually be represented as the underdogs or in need of help. Materials should develop respect for cultural diversity and foster understanding of the customs and traditions of different cultures. They should contain strong positive role models with whom both black and white pupils can identify.

Is The Material Up-To-Date?

Information should be as up-to-date as possible taking into account that societies everywhere are changing, often rapidly, and that to dwell on quaint exotic traditions is not presenting a true picture of life in that society.

Is The Material Biased?
How Accurate Is It?

These questions are clearly linked. Most material has a bias. That is, it has been written from a particular viewpoint (although this is often not recognised by the writer.) Often we will recognise bias only if we disagree with the point of view. Clearly then, it is important to recognise bias and to make sure that the information given is relevant, accurate and balanced. Material which makes sweeping generalisations; simplifies information to the point of distortion; or is prejudiced or bigoted, should be rejected.

Is The Approach Eurocentric/Ethnocentric?

Materials should recognise that other cultures have their own values. These cultures should not be judged through British eyes against British norms. Wherever possible people should be given the opportunity to speak for themselves. The Eurocentric/Ethnocentric approach ignores the developing world viewpoint, tends to show a patronising or condescending attitude and shows Europe as solely 'developing/helping' the poorer countries of the world. The interdependence between peoples and nations, and the influence that actions by one have on the others, need to be clearly shown.

Is The Emphasis Only On The Problems?

There can be a tendency for material to concentrate unduly on the hopelessness and the problems of the developing countries. Whilst these should not be underrated, it is important that positive and hopeful images of people tackling their problems and the sense that individuals have the ability to influence events, are presented.

The aim is not to censor books and materials (although this may be necessary in some instances, for example where emotive language is used) but for teachers to be aware of the varying impressions which can be given and to be prepared to handle and counterbalance false or unbalanced ones. All material will not conform to all criteria. There will be many 'grey' areas. It may not be possible to eliminate entirely 'undesirable' elements from all educational materials, but these can be turned to advantage in educational terms as long as the teacher is aware of them. An important part of children's education is that they should be:

" — made aware of persuasive, manipulative and co-ercive language in story, factual text, the media and advertising.
— taught to recognise national, ethnic, class, sexual, religious and moral bias.
— taught to differentiate between fact and opinion.
— able to infer main ideas not explicitly stated, interpret figurative language, predict outcomes."*

It can therefore be acceptable for children to be exposed to certain elements in the relatively 'controlled' conditions of the classroom, where a system of checks and balances can come into play.

*County of Kent Language Policy Document

Some Useful Resources for Teachers

The selected items listed below, provide basic background information and activity suggestions for teachers. Together they form a very useful bank of reference material for the teacher — the basis of a staff library of resources for the teaching of global development issues. These items can be obtained from the *Centre for World Development Education* along with a comprehensive catalogue of resources. Many other useful resources are available from the addresses listed later.

The Development Puzzle   N. L. Fyson   CWDE/Hodder & Stoughton
Basic handbook for teachers on development issues.

World Studies 8-13, S.   Fisher and D. Hicks   Oliver & Boyd
A practical resource for classroom activities for teachers and in-service.

Teaching World Studies   ed. Hicks and Townley   Longman
An introduction to global perspectives in the curriculum.

Let's Co-operate   M. Masheder   Peace Pledge Union
Ideas and activities handbook for parents and teachers of children aged between 3 and 11, to promote co-operation and peaceful conflict-solving.

Themework: Approaches for Teaching with a Global Perspective   Birmingham Development Education Centre
Wide variety of classroom activities and approaches to themes.

Hidden Messages?   Birmingham Development Education Centre
Activities for exploring bias.

A Sense of School: An Active-Learning Approach to In-Service
Framework for planning and organising in-service workshops.

Earthrights: Education as if the Planet Really Mattered   Global Impact Project
Ideas and activities for primary and secondary classrooms on environmental issues.

Global Teacher, Global Learner   G. Pike and D. Selby   Hodder & Stoughton
Handbook exploring and developing theory and practice of global education with practical activity suggestions.

Whose Paradise? Tea and the Plantation Tamils of Sri Lanka   Minority Rights Group
Resource book on teaching about minority group and human rights issues for primary/lower secondary teachers.

The World Tomorrow   Hampshire D. E. Project 8-13
13 packs for development education topic work. Each pack contains practical approaches to curriculum planning to promote awareness of family, community and global interdependence. Topics: Family Life; Food for Thought; Our School; Celebrations; Living Together; Village Community; A School Exchange; Conservation; Energy; Global Family; On the Move; A Developing Country; A Teacher's Guide.

Children and World Development   R. Williams   UNICEF
Suggests approaches to teaching and learning about development issues, notably women and children in the developing world.

Children's Books for a Multicultural Society 0-7   Books for Children's Books for a Multicultural Society 8-12   Keeps
Critical guides on available books and resources for teachers and librarians.

Assemblies for Development   C.W.D.E.
Fifteen themes on issues of world development for assemblies.

Images of the World: An Introduction to Bias in Teaching Materials D. Hicks   University of London Institute of Education
Textbook images of the developing world.

Teaching About Prejudice   Minority Rights Group
Practical guide to anti-racist practice in schools.

It's Not Fair   Christian Aid
Handbook on world development for youth group leaders.

Starting Together   Birmingham Development Education Centre
Ideas booklet for teachers of young children.

Some Crafty Things To Do   OXFAM
Practical handbook of things for young people to make and do.

Cartoonsheet Discussion Starters   C.W.D.E.
14 Development Topic Sheets on eg. Trade; Aid; Health; Education; Agriculture; Environment; Women; Water, etc. Six-sided foldout cartoon and photo-illustrated information sheets on each topic.

Country Sheets   C.W.D.E.
5 six-sided photo-illustrated sheets on Jamaica; Mali; Sri Lanka; Botswana and Pakistan.

Commodity Sheets   C.W.D.E.
10 six-sided photo-illustrated sheets on Jute; Coffee; Rice; Tea; Wheat; Maize; Copper; Bananas; Tin; Rubber; Sugar.

What Do We Eat? A topic-based program   C.W.D.E. Software
Enables children to analyse their food intake and compare it with that of a different country which they have chosen as their 'project country'.

Water Game   C.W.D.E. Software
A simulation based on the daily use and supply of water.

World Development Database   C.W.D.E. Software/Longman Micro Software
A database containing development data about 125 countries.

Sand Harvest   C.W.D.E. Software/Longman Micro Software
Role play simulation about desertification in the Sahel.

Some Useful Addresses

Contact with the selected addresses listed overleaf, will provide:

1. useful classroom resources — books, posters/wallcharts, audio-visual aids, games and simulations, — for teaching the global perspective.

2. information on specific topics and themes.

3. advice and help in planning topics and themes.

4. advice and help with school-focus in-service training on world development issues and

5. *in some cases* help in facilitating classroom activities.

Action Aid
Highgate Hill
London N19 5PS

Africa Centre
38 King Street
London WC2E 8JT

Afro-Caribbean Education Resource Project
Centre for Learning Resources
275 Kennington Lane
London SE11 5QZ

Catholic Fund for Overseas Development (CAFOD)
2 Romero Close
Stockwell Road
London SW9 9TY

Centre for World Development Education
Regents College
Inner Circle
Regents Park
London NW1 4NS

Christian Aid
PO Box 100
London SE1 7RT

Commonwealth Institute
Kensington High Street
London W8 6NQ

ILEA Centre for Learning Resources
275 Kennington Lane
London SE11 5QZ

Latin American Bureau
1 Amwell Street
London EC1R 1UL

National Association of Development Education Centres (NADEC)
6 Endsleigh Street
London WC1H 0DX
(Network of Local Development Education Centres — list on request)

OXFAM
274 Banbury Road
Oxford OX2 7DZ
(Network of Local Youth and Education Staff)

Save The Children Fund
Mary Datchelor House
17 Grove Lane
London SE5 8RD

SOAS Extra Mural Division
Malet Street
London W1

UNICEF
55 Lincoln's Inn Fields
London WC2A 3NB

War on Want
Three Castles House
1 London Bridge Street
London SE1 9SG

Water Aid
1 Queen Anne's Gate
London SW1H 9BT

World Wide Fund for Nature (WWF)
Panda House
Wayside Park
Godalming
Surrey GU7 1XR

APPENDIX I
TOPICS AND CONCEPTS "READY RECKONER"

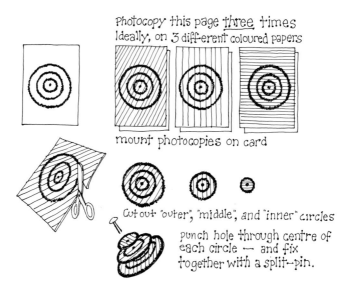

Photocopy this page three times
Ideally, on 3 different coloured papers

mount photocopies on card

Cut out "outer", "middle", and "inner" circles

punch hole through centre of each circle — and fix together with a split-pin.

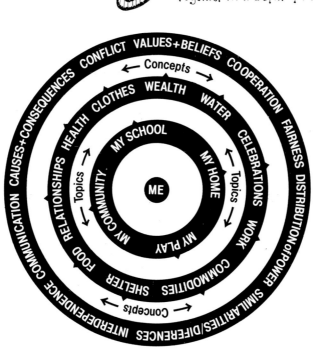

APPENDIX II

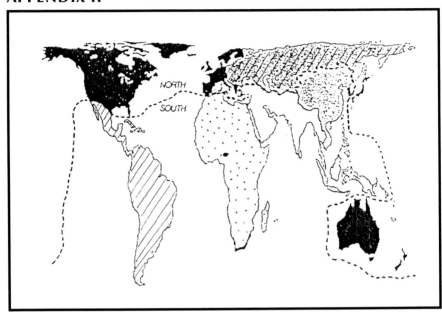

30 children to represent the World's population.
66 sweets to represent the World's food distribution.
(e.g. USSR — 1 child with 3 sweets; North America — 2 children with
2 + 5 sweets)

NORTH
AMERICA
②⑤

USSR
③

EUROPE
②③
③④

CHINA ②
②②②②
②②

LATIN
AMERICA
①
②④

AFRICA
①⓪
②③

ASIA
①③②②
②①②
①

OCEANA
+ JAPAN
③